WATER

BookLife

Written by
Harriet Brundle

©2017
Book Life
King's Lynn
Norfolk PE30 4LS

ISBN: 978-1-786370-37-2

All rights reserved
Printed in Malaysia

Written by:
Harriet Brundle

Edited by:
Grace Jones

Designed by:
Danielle Jones

A catalogue record for this book
is available from the British Library.

Contents

Page	Title
4–5	What is a Material?
6–7	What is Water?
8–9	Properties of Water
10–11	Freezing Water
12–13	Heating Water
14–15	Uses of Water
16–17	The Water Cycle
18–19	Water Around the World
20–21	Saving Water
22	Fun Facts
23	Glossary
24	Index

The red words in this book can be found in the glossary on page 23.

What is a Material?

Materials are what things are made of. Some materials are natural and some are man-made.

Water

Wood

Rock

Glass

Plastic

Metal

Every material has its own properties. A material might be very soft. This would be one of its properties.

Pyjamas, cuddly toys and pillows are all soft.

What is Water?

Water is a natural material that is mostly found in seas, rivers, lakes and below the ground. It is a liquid that has no smell and is transparent.

Water is an extremely important material. It covers 70% of the Earth's surface and all living things need it to live.

Did you know?
Around 60% of an adult's body is water!

Properties of Water

Water can either be a solid, a liquid or a gas. When water is solid, it is called ice. If ice is thick, it is hard and very stiff. Ice feels extremely cold to the touch.

BE CAREFUL!
Ice can be slippery!

Liquid water takes the shape of the space it is given. For example, when you pour water into a glass, it takes the shape of the glass.

When water is a gas, it is called steam. Steam can be very hot to touch!

Freezing Water

When water is colder than 0 degrees Celsius, it freezes and becomes ice. Water that has salt in it, for example sea water, can usually only freeze at much colder temperatures.

Celsius is a measure of temperature.

When the weather is cold enough, rain water will freeze as it falls to the ground. When this happens, it is snowing!

Did you know?
There is ice on the planet Mars.

Heating Water

When water is heated to a temperature of 100 degrees Celsius, it becomes a gas called steam. This process is called evaporation.

We can measure the temperature of something by using a thermometer.

Steam is made out of tiny droplets of water and it looks like white mist. When the droplets cool, they turn back into liquid.

Uses of Water

We use water for lots of different things every day.

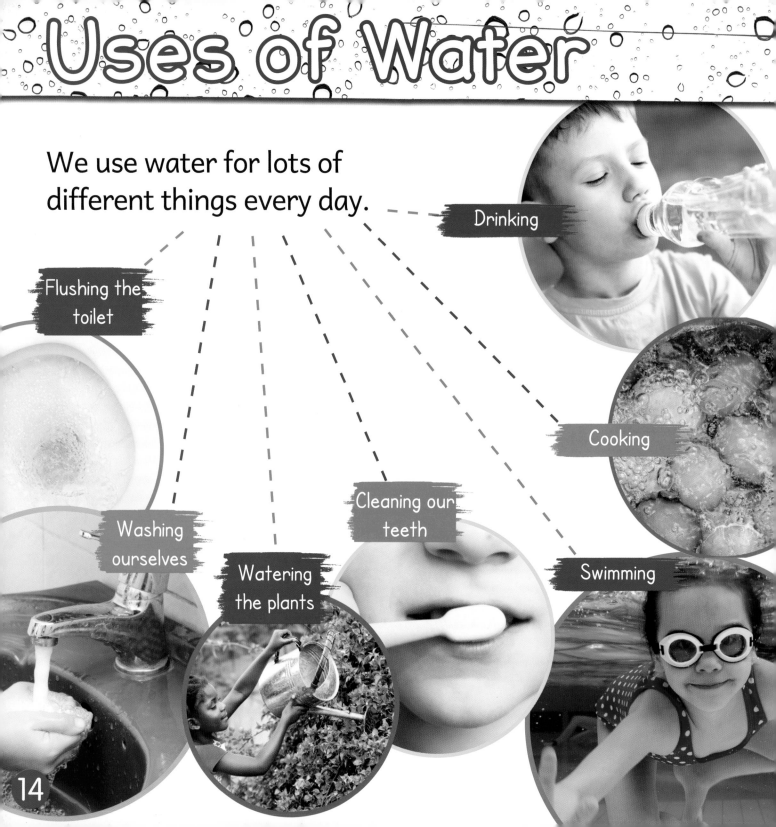

Drinking

Flushing the toilet

Cooking

Washing ourselves

Watering the plants

Cleaning our teeth

Swimming

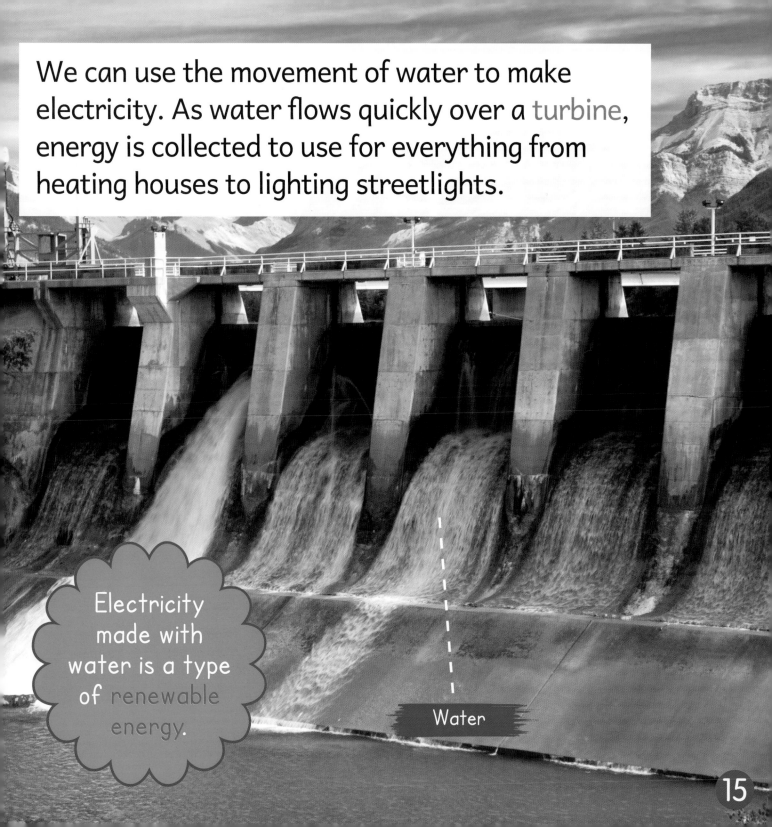

We can use the movement of water to make electricity. As water flows quickly over a turbine, energy is collected to use for everything from heating houses to lighting streetlights.

Electricity made with water is a type of renewable energy.

Water

The Water Cycle

When the sun shines on water, the heat from the sun turns some of the water into a very light steam, which is called water vapour.

Sunshine

Water Vapour

The water vapour travels up into the air. When it cools down, it falls as rain and the water cycle starts again.

Rain

Water Around the World

Angel Falls in the country of Venezuela is the tallest waterfall in the world. The water drops 807 metres before it hits the ground!

The River Nile in Africa is the longest river in the world; it is over 4,000 miles long.

Many people live next to the River Nile and use the water to help them to grow crops.

Saving Water

There is a limited amount of water on Earth, so it is important that we do not waste it. There are lots of different ways that we can reduce the amount of water that we use.

We can turn off the tap when brushing our teeth, use the shower for less time and use a watering can instead of a hosepipe to water the plants in the garden.

Can you think of any other ways we can help to save water?

Fun Facts

Cucumbers are 95% water!

The average person uses around 150 litres of water every day.

Glacier

Ice Cap

Most of the Earth's fresh water drink is frozen in polar ice caps and glaciers.

Glossary

Limited
a small amount.

Man-made
something that is made or caused by humans.

Natural
something that has been made by nature.

Properties
the different qualities of a material.

Reduce
make smaller in amount or size.

Renewable energy
a type of energy that can be used again and again without running out.

Transparent
see-through.

Turbine
a type of machine that liquid flows through to make power.

Index

Earth 7, 20, 22

Evaporation 12

Freeze 10–11

Gas 8-9, 12

Liquid 6, 8–9, 13

Rain 11, 17

Rivers 6, 19

Seas 6, 10

Solid 8

Sun 16

Temperature 10, 12

Water Cycle 16–17

Photocredits: Abbreviations: l-left, r-right, b-bottom, t-top, c-centre, m-middle.
Front cover t - Rich Carey Front Cover m – Aleksandar Mijatovic Front cover b – Kirill Smirnov. 1 – Kirill Smirnov. 2 – Aleksandar Mijatovic. 3 – Serg64. 4 – Sunny studio. 4 – YanLev 4tl – Sunny studio 4bl – 3445128471 4m – Temych 4br – 4tr – Pressmaster. 5l – wavebreakmedia. 5r – hartphotography. 6l – Songchai W 6tr – Songquan Deng 6br – zbindere. 7 – Maxim Blinkov. 8r – Serg Zastavkin 8l – Bull's-Eye Arts. 9l – Toa55 9r – Gyvafoto. 10l – Valentyn Volkov 10r – DonLand. 11l – jonson 11r – Vadim Sadovski. 12l – VladisChern 12r – Roman Sigaev. 13 – kazoka. 14tl – Lenor Ko 14bl – wckiw 14cl – Lucian Coman 14cr – stopabox 14br Anton Balazh 14mr – Pollapat Chirawong 14tr – sakkmesterke. 15 – Constantine Androsoff. 16l – Triff. 16r – Doug McLean. 17 – thegiffary. 18c – Alice Nerr 18m – posteriori. 19 – Elzbieta Sekowska. 20 – Matic Stojs. 21 – Zoom Team. 21b – zentilia. 22l – Romolo Tavani 22t – Monebook 22m – Galyna Andrushko 22br – Marcel Clemens. 24 – VaLiza.
Images are courtesy of Shutterstock.com. With thanks to Getty Images, Thinkstock Photo and iStockphoto.